Are you ready for an Art Attack?

Over the next few pages you'll discover some **brand new** Art Attacks to keep you busy!

Find out how you can turn ordinary household rubbish and packaging into **unique** things to organise, decorate and delight! So, roll your sleeves up, turn the page and let's have an Art Attack...

CONTENTS

Editor: Karen Brown
Junior Designer: Darren Miles
Designer: Antony Gardner
Prop maker: Susie Johns

D0774266

SNAP HAPPY!

Make sure you're always in the picture with this cool camera photo holder – the perfect accessory for those with a flair for photography!

1 From thick cardboard, cut two rectangles 18cm x 12cm for the front and back, one measuring 12cm x 3cm for the side and two measuring 18cm x 3cm for the top and base. Stick them together with sticky tape. One side will be left open. Use the picture as a guide.

3cm

18cm

12cm

2  Paste a couple layers of newspaper strips soaked in diluted PVA glue all over the joins. Leave to dry thoroughly overnight.

PVA

3 Cut out an oval of card and stick it to the front. Using PVA, stick a jam jar lid and then a plastic lid on top to make the lens. Stick a rectangle of card on for a flash and another small lid for the shutter release button.

PVA

4

Cardboard box
card, sticky tape,
card, jam jar lid,
2 plastic lids,
newspaper, PVA
glue, paints, string,
black marker pen.

4

Paint the camera silver or black. Leave the
bottle tops unpainted. When the paint is
dry, stick a black circle of paper with little
yellow marks on it to the lens (plastic lid)
to make it more realistic. Add details with
a black or silver marker pen.

When dry, make a hole
either side and push some
string though. Finally,
slip some special snaps
in the middle!

AUTO FLASH

ultra Zoom

ADVANCED   2002

SHELL SHOCKED!

This terrific tortoise will slow you down when you want to spend, spend, spend! Save up for something special with this cute money box!

1 To make the shell, blow up a balloon and cover half of it with at least 8 layers of torn newspaper strips pasted on with diluted PVA glue. Leave to dry.

2 Burst the balloon. Trim the shell, then place it on a piece of card and draw round it. Cut this out and tape it to the shell.

3 Stick a cut down kitchen roll tube on for a neck. Attach a scrunched up ball of newspaper to this for the head. Add a rolled up piece of card for the tail and 4 pieces of card for the feet.

4 Cover the tortoise with another 3 layers of papier maché and leave to dry. Then carefully cut a slot in the shell for money. (Cut a small hole in the shell at the back so you can remove the money.)

PVA

5 Finally paint your tortoise. Add a funny face using black marker pen. How about making a card hat to make him extra cute!

SAILOR SKITTLES

These super skittles are great for playing indoors or out with a few of your friends. So start collecting those plastic bottles if you want to be bowled over!

Wash and dry all your empty plastic bottles. Attach a scrunched up paper ball to the top of each bottle using sticky tape to make the heads.

Cover each skittle with 3 or 4 layers of torn newspaper pasted on with diluted PVA glue. For the heads and necks you may prefer to use kitchen paper. Leave to dry overnight in a warm place.

When they're completely dry, paint them. Start by painting them all white to cover up the newspaper print. Leave them to dry again.

YOU CAN USE DIFFERENT SIZED OR SHAPED BOTTLES IF YOU PREFER. YOU CAN EVEN PAINT THEM AS DIFFERENT CHARACTERS. WHAT ABOUT A FEW PIRATES?

4

Then use bright colours and add detail with black marker pen. Paint 5 skittles like sailors and the sixth one as the captain, using the picture as a guide.

I bet you've got loads of books – well these brilliant piggy bookends will cheer up any shelf! So get stuck in!

1 Blow up a round balloon and cover it with at least 8 layers of torn newspaper pasted on with diluted PVA glue. Leave to dry.

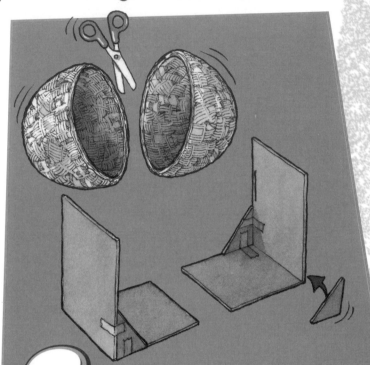

2 Burst the balloon and cut the shell in half. Cut two L shapes pieces from a smallish box. Stick on small triangles at the front to give it strength.

3 Tape rolled up pieces of card on to one half of the shell to make front legs. Tape a paper cup in place for a snout and add rolled up card for the lower jaw. Stick on card ears and some rolled up newspaper to form a brow.

4 Tape rolled up pieces of card on to the other half to make back legs. Add a thinly rolled piece of paper for a tail. Then stick both halves on to the L shaped card ends.

MUD!?

5

Cover both halves with 4 layers of papier maché, keeping it as smooth as possible. Then paint! Paint the pig pink and the base green. Add some brown for mud!

PERFECT POST

Keep in touch with this super stationary organiser. But watch out –
as soon as your mum and dad see it, they'll want one too!

1 Cut out pieces of card from thick cardboard. The front piece is 22cm x 7.5cm, the back is 22cm x 18cm, the middle is 22cm x 12.5cm, the base is 23cm x 11cm and the two side pieces are 7.5cm x 10cm x 18cm.

side
back — 22cm, 18cm
side
middle — 22cm, 12.5cm
base — 11cm, 23cm
front — 22cm

2 Tape the pieces together like this. Then cover with three layers of torn newspaper strips pasted on with PVA glue. Leave to dry.

PVA

3 Paint the rack white all over and leave to dry. Then decorate as you wish. How about some Art Attack splats?

BOX!

Darren Miles,

HOT TIPS

Why not use old stamps, stickers or photos to decorate your post box?

Cover the whole thing with a layer of PVA glue after you have finished decorating. This will protec the paint and give it a shiny finish.

MOVING MUSIC

Keep all your latest CDs in this terrific truck built for the job!
Just wheel it over to the CD player - keep all your energy for dancing!

1 Cut off one short end of a shoebox and then cut the sides diagonally. Take the cereal box and stuff it with newspaper to make it strong. Tape the ends down. Stick the shoebox to the cereal box.

2 Turn the boxes upside down. Cut two pieces of corrugated card the same width as the box and about 7cm wide. Stick in place to form axles for the wheels.

3 To make the cab, cut the sides from a square tissue box like this. Cut a strip of corrugated card to fit over the top. Tape two smaller boxes to the bottom.

4 Attach the cab to the back. Cover the whole thing with 5 layers of papier maché. Pay attention to the joins and leave the axles open. While this is drying, get another box to fit inside as the CD container.

MUSIC ON THE MOVE!

5. Now paint the whole thing. When dry stick lids on for lights and add detail in black pen. What about sticking on a label and some CDs?

6 Make four wheels from thick card and make holes in the middle. Get two sticks, slightly longer than the width of the truck. Stick a wheel on one end, push it through the axle and stick the other wheel on. Paint the wheels.

WIZARD'S KIT!

If magic is your thing, you'll need the outfit! Start by creating this important kit for young apprentice wizards!

POINTY HAT

1 Make a cone shape big enough to fit your head. Draw a larger circle around it onto card to make the brim.

2 Cut out a smaller circle with tabs all the way around it. Tape the cone to the brim using the tabs to secure it in place.

3 Cover with four layers of papier maché. Crumple the hat slightly to give it a bit of character. Let dry and then paint purple with pink stars. Finally brush with glue and sprinkle with glitter.

PVA

TWIG WAND

YOU WILL NEED: newspaper, sticky tape, kitchen paper, PVA glue, paint.

1 Roll newspaper into a tight sausage, tape in place and trim. Scrunch up kitchen paper, dip in diluted PVA glue and stick to your wand, to make knobbly bits. Cover with four layers of papier maché. Leave to dry, then paint to look like a twig!

1 Blow up the balloon to the size you want. Brush with diluted PVA glue and cover with 8 layers of torn newspaper strips. Leave to dry.

POTION POT

YOU WILL NEED: Balloon, PVA glue, newspapers, scissors, cardboard, sticky tape, acrylic paints, wire or string.

2 Burst the balloon and trim the papier maché shell to make a bowl shape. To make the 3 legs, roll some cardboard into tubes and tape to the bottom.

3 Cover the legs with three layers of papier maché. Let dry and then paint. Dab with bronze and black paint to make the cauldron look like it's made of old iron! Make a handle from wire or string.

17

STRUMMING ALON

Fancy yourself as a rock or pop star? Well get practicing your air guitar! Get your friends to make instruments too and you can form a band!

YOU WILL NEED:
Cardboard box card, sticky tape, newspaper, PVA glue, paints, string, 3 straws, pins.

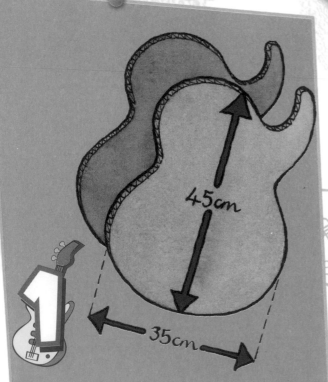

1 45cm 35cm

Cut two guitar shapes from cardboard about 45cms long and 35cm wide at the widest point.

2 4.5 cm 53cm 75 cm

Cut 3 strips of card, two 53cm long and 4.5cm wide and one 75cm long and 4.5cm wide. Stick them together in a prism shape with the longest piece on the bottom.

3

Cut a strip of corrugated card 4.5cm wide and long enough to go round the guitar shape. Stick this in between the shapes taping it to both edges. Stick a small rectangle of card (10.5cm x 3.5cm) the front.

4·5cm

4

8cm

15cm

Stick the longest part of fret board to the front. Cut out a piece of cardboard 15cm x 8cm. Cut the corners off and curve the sides. Stick this to the end of the fret board sandwiching three cut down straws in between.

5

Cover the whole thing with four layers of papier maché and leave to dry. Cover with white paint and then bright colours.

PVA

6

Finally add your strings. Use elastic, string or thread. Attach to the top and bottom of the fret board with glue or drawing pins.

BEAR NECESS

1 Wash and dry your empty plastic bottle. Then fill it with sand or gravel and screw the lid back on tightly.

2 Stick a cut down toilet roll on for a neck. Scrunch up a ball of newspaper to make a head. Roll up pieces of corrugated card to form two arms. Tape on cardboard ears and a plastic bottle top for a snout.

3
Cover your bear with 4 layers of papier maché paying attention to the joins. Leave to dry in a warm place. near a radiator or in the airing cupboard would be good.

4 Paint your bear any way you like. How about painting a pair of jeans and a t-shirt like this? Add a cute face with black marker pen.

ITY!

THIS TEDDY BEAR DOORSTOP MAY NOT BE CUDDLY BUT HE'LL CERTAINLY BRIGHTEN UP YOUR ROOM. USE HIM TO KEEP ANY DOOR OPEN AND WELCOME FRIENDS IN!

YOU CAN DESIGN ANY SORT OF DOORSTOP YOU LIKE. FROM ANIMALS TO PEOPLE OR MONSTERS - A PLASTIC BOTTLE MAKES A GREAT STARTING POINT. TRY IT YOURSELF!

YOU WILL NEED:

Large plastic bottle with lid, sand or small pebbles, newspaper, cardboard, sticky tape, plastic lid, PVA glue, paints.

HOT TIP!

You can make feet if you want. Simply stick on a feet shaped piece of card in step 2. Build the feet up with scrunched up balls of newspaper and then cover with paper maché in step 3. Finally paint shoes on!

OCEAN VIEW!

Make your favourite pictures or photos stand out by putting them in this marvellous marine frame!

1 Start by making a sturdy frame. Cut the frame shape from thick cardboard box card. Stick several pieces together to make it really strong.

2 Cover the frame with about three layers of torn newspaper pasted on with diluted PVA glue, wrapping strips of paper round the frame, covering all the edges. Leave to dry.

PVA

3 Cut out fish, starfish and seaweed shapes from cardboard. Cover them with two layers of papier maché and leave to dry.

PVA

4 Glue the shapes on to the frame and cover with another layer of papier maché. when dry, paint the frame white all over. Then paint as you wish.

DOWN TO EARTH!

Recycle in style with this wicked waste bin! Use it to save things for making Art Attacks or collect stuff for recycling bins.

1 Cut the 4 sides and base from cardboard box card. Each side measures 32cm high with a top edge of 27cm and a base of 16cm. Cut out a base for the bin measuring 16cm square.

27cm

32cm

16cm

16cm

16cm

2 Tape the pieces together firmly like this and then tape an upside down paper plate to one side.

3 Cover the bin, inside and out, with at least three layers of torn newspaper pasted on with diluted PVA glue. Leave to dry thoroughly.

PVA

4 Paint the whole thing white and then decorate any colour you wish. Paint the plate to look like Earth and add an appropriate slogan.

Cardboard, sticky tape, newspaper, PVA glue, paints.

save the

PLANET

ART ATTACK

HINTS AND TIPS!

Papier maché actually means chewed paper! It is a great way to mould, model and make fantastic Art Attacks! Below you'll find some suggestions to help you become a success with papier maché.

PAPER

You can use all sorts of paper to make papier maché including tissue paper, kitchen roll, magazine paper or newspaper. Newspaper is the best and cheapest - you can achieve quite smooth results. Kitchen roll is better for creating pulp - soggy, mashed up paper - which is great for creating small details and features.

BALLOON

Balloons are a vital component in your papier maché kit! You can make hundreds of things from the shell created by covering all or half of it with papier maché. When covering the balloon, use a bowl to support it. Cover half the balloon with papier maché, turn it over and then do the other half.

PAINT

Acrylic paint is best for painting on textured models and papier maché. You will need to give your model a coat of white paint first to cover the newspaper print.

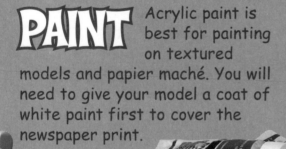

GLUE

When your model is dry, cover it with a layer of PVA glue. This will give it a lovely, shiny finish and protect the paint.

PVA glue can be used for fixing things together, making the papier maché mixture and varnishing.

Always read the instructions on the glue. You'll find that you'll need to mix the PVA glue in equal parts with water or 2 parts PVA to 1 part water to get a good consistency.